THE PRIVATE DINING-ROOM
AND OTHER NEW VERSES

ALDINE PAPERBACKS

OGDEN NASH

THE PRIVATE DINING-ROOM

AND OTHER NEW VERSES

J. M. DENT & SONS LTD

Made in Great Britain
at the
Aldine Press · Letchworth · Herts
for
J. M. DENT & SONS LTD
Aldine House · Bedford Street · London
First published in U.S.A. 1952
First published in Great Britain 1953
Reprinted 1953
Paperback edition 1964

FOR NELL

the only grandchild

in the world

Some of these verses first appeared in the following magazines and are reprinted through the courtesy of *Vogue, Good Housekeeping, Look, Flair, House and Garden, Harper's, The Saturday Evening Post, What's New, Glamour, The New Yorker, Life, Cosmopolitan,* and *Woman's Day.*

CONTENTS

THE PRIVATE DINING-ROOM

Miss Rafferty wore taffeta,
Miss Cavendish wore lavender.
We ate pickerel and mackerel
And other lavish provender.
Miss Cavendish was Lalage,
Miss Rafferty was Barbara.
We gobbled pickled mackerel
And broke the candelabara,
Miss Cavendish in lavender,
In taffeta, Miss Rafferty,
The girls in taffeta lavender,
And we, of course, in mufti.

Miss Rafferty wore taffeta,
The taffeta was lavender,
Was lavend, lavender, lavenderest,
As the wine improved the provender.
Miss Cavendish wore lavender,
The lavender was taffeta.
We boggled mackled pickerel,
And bumpers did we quaffeta.
And Lalage wore lavender,
And lavender wore Barbara,
Rafferta taffeta Cavender lavender
Barbara abracadabra.

Miss Rafferty in taffeta
Grew definitely raffisher.
Miss Cavendish in lavender
Grew less and less stand-offisher.

With Lalage and Barbara
We grew a little pickereled,
We ordered Mumm and Roederer
Because the bubbles tickereled.
But lavender and taffeta
Were gone when we were soberer.
I haven't thought for thirty years
Of Lalage and Barbara.

PEEKABOO, I ALMOST SEE YOU

Middle-aged life is merry, and I love to lead it,
But there comes a day when your eyes are all right but your arm isn't long enough to hold the telephone book where you can read it,
And your friends get jocular, so you go to the oculist,
And of all your friends he is the joculist,
So over his facetiousness let us skim,
Only noting that he has been waiting for you ever since you said Good evening to his grandfather clock under the impression that it was him,
And you look at his chart and it says SHRDLU QWERTYOP, and you say Well, why SHRDNTLU QWERTYOP? and he says one set of glasses won't do.
You need two,
One for reading Erle Stanley Gardner's *Perry Mason* and Keats's *Endymion* with,
And the other for walking around without saying Hallo to strange wymion with.
So you spend your time taking off your seeing glasses to put on your reading glasses, and then remembering that your reading glasses are upstairs or in the car,
And then you can't find your seeing glasses again because without them you can't see where they are.
Enough of such mishaps, they would try the patience of an ox,
I prefer to forget both pairs of glasses and pass my declining years saluting strange women and grandfather clocks.

CORRECTION: *EVE* DELVED AND *ADAM* SPAN

The ladies of the garden club
Are in the other room,
And, fed on tea and sandwiches,
Their pretty fancies bloom.
I hear their gentle treble hubbub,
The ladies of the garden clubbub.

The ladies of the garden club,
Their words are firm and sure,
They know the lore of lime and mulch,
The poetry of manure.
Each spring they beautify our suburb,
The ladies of the garden cluburb.

Dear ladies of the garden club,
I love your natural zeal,
Your verdant thumbs, your canvas gloves,
The pads on which you kneel,
But I hear you making plans involving
Husbands in gardening instead of golfing.

Between the outer door and me
The flower ladies sit.
I 'm frantic-footed, blind, and trapped,
Like mole in compost pit,
One timorous masculine minutia,
Caught between baby's-breath and fuchsia.

The air is sweet with talk of bulbs,
And phlox and mignonettes;
Arrangements drape the drawer that holds
My only cigarettes.
Would I had courage for an end run
Round herbaceous border and rhododendron!

Ranunculus can a prison make,
And hyacinth a cell;
I barely glimpse a patch of sky
Through wreath of immortelle.
And thus are fulfilled the baleful prophecies
Concerning men who are at home instead of their offices.

MY TRIP DAORBA

I have just returned from a foreign tour,
But ask me not what I saw, because I am not sure.
Not being a disciplinarian like Father Day,
I saw everything the wrong way,
Because of one thing about Father Day I am sure,
Which is that he would not have ridden backwards so that the little Days could ride forwards on their foreign tour.
Indeed I am perhaps the only parent to be found
Who saw Europe, or eporuE, as I think of it, the wrong way round.
I added little to my knowledge of the countryside but much to my reputation for docility
Riding backwards through ecnarF and ylatI.
I am not quite certain,
But I think in siraP I saw the ervuoL, the rewoT leffiE, and the Cathedral of emaD ertoN.
I shall remember ecnerolF for ever,
For that is where I backed past the house where etnaD wrote the 'onrefnI,' or ydemoC eniviD, and twisted my neck admiring the bridges across the onrA reviR.
In emoR I glimpsed the muroF and the nacitaV as in a mirror in the fog,
While in ecineV I admired the ecalaP s'egoD as beheld from the steerage of an alodnoG.
So I find conditions overseas a little hard to judge,
Because all I know is what I saw retreating from me as I rode backwards in compartments in the niart and in carriages sitting on the taes-pmuj.

THE ANNIVERSARY

A marriage aged one
Is hardly begun;
A fling in the sun,
But it 's hardly begun;
A green horse,
A stiff course,
And leagues to be run.

A marriage aged five
Is coming alive.
Watch it wither and thrive;
Though it 's coming alive,
You must guess,
No or yes,
If it 's going to survive.

A marriage aged ten
Is a hopeful Amen;
It 's pray for it then,
And mutter Amen,
As the names
Of old flames
Sound again and again.

At twenty a marriage
Discovers its courage.
This year do not disparage,
It is comely in courage;
Past the teens,
And blue jeans,
It 's a promising marriage.

Yet before twenty-one
It has hardly begun.
How tall in the sun,
Yet hardly begun!
But once come of age,
Pragmatically sage,
Oh, blithe to engage
Is sweet marri-age.

Tilt a twenty-first cup
To a marriage grown up,
Now sure and mature,
And securely grown up.
Raise twenty-one cheers
To the silly young years,
While I sit out the dance
With my dearest of dears.

ALL, ALL ARE GONE, THE OLD FAMILIAR QUOTATIONS

Who was born too soon? I will tell you who was born too soon: Francis Bacon, Baron Verulam.
Therefore he could not ask his friends: 'Why is Charles Lamb like Baltimore,' and supply his own answer: 'Because he is deep in the heart of Mary Lamb.'
Who was born too late? I will tell you without further parley:
It was I, because I cannot remember whether it was Charles Lamb or who, who on the death of his last nearest and dearest pathetically exclaimed: 'Now there is no one left to call me Charlie.'
I am always getting entangled in such mnemonic snarls,
But from internal evidence it was obviously someone named Charles,
So it couldn't have been Scrooge or Marley.
Nor could it have been Charles II, because there was always somebody to call him Charlie.
It would have been duck soup or pie or jam
If he had said: 'There is no one left to call me Elia,' then I would have known it was Lamb.
If I could but spot a conclusion, I should race to it,
But Charles is such a simple name that I can't put a face to it.
Still, I shouldn't complain, since it is its simplicity that gives it its pathos;
There would be no poignancy in saying: 'There is no one left to call me Charlemagne or Lancelot or Athos.'

People prefer the simple to the grandiose,
And I do not believe that even in an antique land anybody would sympathize with anybody who went around saying: 'There is no one left to call me Ozymandias.'

EVERYBODY LOVES A BRIDE, EVEN THE GROOM

Blessings on the bonnie bride,
I gaze upon her starry-eyed.
Brides are girls on whom I dote,
They bring a lump into my throat.
At the sound of Mendelssohn and Wagner
My spirit swoops like a tobogganer.

Beneath the shimmering bridal veil
Tomboys look demure and pale,
Hoydens turn into paragons,
And downy ducklings into swans.
I wish the Archbishop of Westminster
Would make a bride of every spinster.

Bless the bravely trousseau'd wife
Honeymooning into life.
Instead of showers of shoes and rice
Let us give her good advice.
Give it, and quickly dodge aside—
Have you ever tried to guide a bride?

Dear bride, remember, if you can,
That thing you married is a man.
His thoughts are low, his mind is earthy,
Of you he is totally unworthy;
Wherein lies a lesson too few have larnt it—
That 's the reason you married him, aren't it?

The organ booms, the procession begins,
The rejected suitors square their chins,
And angels swell the harmonious tide
Of blessings upon the bonnie bride.
But blessings also on him without whom
There would be no bride. I mean the groom.

THE HAPPY ENDING OF MR TRAIN

Once there was a man named Mr Train who wasn't called Choo-choo, which in itself is odd.
Furthermore, he knew a Mr Rhodes who wasn't called Dusty, and a Mr Sloan who wasn't called Tod.
And they felt very unpopular not to be called Tod and Dusty and Choo-choo,
Because this was back in the days when if you were popular you were called Stinky or Baldy or the Tennessee Shad, and chicle had just replaced tobacco as the new chew.
Well, of their unpopularity they grew wearier and wearier,
Until they got together and decided that they were unpopular because they were superior,
And Mr Sloan was asked by Mr Rhodes, and Mr Train, who kept going CHOO-choo, CHOO-choo, CHOO-choo, choo-CHOO,
Just how superior are YOU?
And Mr Sloan replied that even as a child he had been familiar with Homer's *Iliad* and Xenophon's *Anabasis*,
And he knew that the classical word for a clump of trees was coppice, so that he always went over the river and into the clump of trees to play coppice and robberses,
And Mr Rhodes and Mr Train said You are still unpopular and alone,
You are not Tod, or even 's Liniment, you are still just Mr Sloan.

And the aesthetic Mr Rhodes boasted, I am superior because to my fiancée who to marry me was waiting until I got a steady job I said It 's not too good, it 's truly too bad you waited,
Because I did have a steady job teaching Art for seven years, but Art just graduated.
And Mr Sloan retired at once to his coppices and bosky abodes,
Murmuring, No Dusty he, nor even the Colossus of, he was born, lived, and will die, as Mr Rhodes.
But Mr Train, he ain't say nuffin'
Just set on de sidin', a-tootin' and a-puffin'.

THE CALENDAR-WATCHERS
or
WHAT'S SO WONDERFUL ABOUT BEING A PATRIARCH?

I'm like a backward berry
Unripened on the vine,
For all my friends are fifty
And I'm only forty-nine.

My friends are steeped in wisdom,
Like senators they go,
In the light of fifty candles,
And one on which to grow.

How can I cap their sallies,
Or top their taste in wine?
Matched with the worldly fifties,
What chance has forty-nine?

Behold my old companions,
My playmates and my peers,
Remote on the Olympus
Of half a hundred years!

These grave and reverend seniors,
They call me Little Man,
They pat my head jocosely
And pinch my cheek of tan.

Why must I scuff my loafers
And grin a schoolboy grin?
Is not my waist as ample?
Is not my hair as thin?

When threatened with a rumba,
Do I not seek the bar?
And am I not the father
Of a freshman at Bryn Mawr?

O, wad some pawky power
Gie me a gowden giftie,
I 'd like to stop at forty-nine,
But pontificate like fifty.

Mine is a dauntless spirit, meaning a spirit that is hard to daunt;
Therefore, since nobody gives me Christmas presents any more, I shall console myself by compiling a list of Christmas presents that I do not want.
I do not want a lamp made out of an umbrella stand, or a coffee-table made out of an old wagon-wheel, or a fire-screen made out of a leftover piece of trellis,
Or, indeed, anything made out of, or to look like, anything ellis.
I do not want a novel written by a young genius in the earnest belief that nothing awful has ever happened before to anyone but him, certainly not to us dowdy duffers and stodgy codgers,
Nor tickets to the new musical by the smart boys who think they have discovered the secret of Hammerstein and Rodgers.
Since I am crazy about harshness and unpleasant aftertaste, I do not want a milder, less irritating cigarette, no matter how scientific the tests,
Nor an evening with friends watching the T.V. personality girls whom I can only think of irreverently as Community Chests.
I do not want a squirrel tail or a Confederate flag to dangle from the aerial of my car,
Or a picture window through which better to view my neighbour's picture window or the adjacent abattoir.
For me, please, no bottled Martinis,

No sweetbreads, no cottage cheese with or without chives, no blinis in sour cream, indeed, neither sour cream nor blinis.
If you will just not come across with any one of the above, and make it snappy.
You will also make one dear old gentleman's Christmas very, very happy.

FLOW GENTLY, SWEET ETYMOLOGY, ORNITHOLOGY, AND PENOLOGY

Pronounce the Nightingale in Persian;
It comes out Bulbul in their version.
Thus every convict in Iran
Feels kinship with some Ossining man,
For be it summer-sing or spring-sing,
He loves to hear the Bulbul sing sing.

A CAUTION TO HILLBILLY SINGERS, HARPISTS, HARPOONISTS, CHANNEL-SWIMMERS, AND PEOPLE FIRST IN LINE FOR WORLD SERIES TICKETS

Fame was a claim of Uncle Ed's,
Simply because he had three heads,
Which, if he'd only had a third of,
I think he would never have been heard of.

A CAUTION TO EVERYBODY

Consider the auk;
Becoming extinct because he forgot how to fly, and
could only walk.
Consider man, who may well become extinct
Because he forgot how to walk and learned how to fly
before he thinked.

THE SNAKE, WITHOUT WHOM ADAM WOULD NEVER HAVE LOOKED AT THE LADY ONCE

Girls cry, upon the sight of snakes,
Faugh, Ugh, also, For heaven's sakes!
Thus many, many boys get kissed,
Which, without snakes, they might have missed.

SHOO, SHOO, SHOEMAKER

I often grieve for Uncle Hannibal
Who inadvertently became a cannibal.
He asked Aunt Mary to roast him the gobbler;
She understood him to say, the cobbler.

I DIDN'T SAY A WORD
or
WHO CALLED THAT PICCOLO PLAYER A FATHER?

A man could be granted to live a dozen lives,
And he still wouldn't understand daughters and wives.
It may be because sometimes their ears are pierced for
earrings,
But they have the most eccentric hearings.
Their hearings are in fact so sensitive
That you frequently feel reprehensitive.
At home, for instance, when near you,
Nobody can hear you.
After your most brilliant fireside or breakfast-table chats
you can count on two fingers the responses you will
have got:
Either, Don't mumble, dear, or, more simply,
What?
I suppose if you're male and parental
You get used to being treated mental,
But you'd feel less psychically distant
If they weren't so inconsistent,
Because if you open your mouth in a hotel or a
restaurant their eardrums quiver at every decibel,
And their embarrassment is almost, if not quite, in-
exprecibel.
Their eyes signal What's cooking? at you,
And their lips hiss, Shush, Daddy, everybody's look-
ing at you!
Now, I realize that old age is a thing of beauty,
Because I have read Cicero's *De Senectute*,

But I prefer to approach senility in my own way, so I 'll thank nobody to rush me,
By which I mean specifically that my voice in a tea-room is no louder than anybody else's, so why does everybody have to shush me?

THERE'S A LAW, ISN'T THERE?
or
I CAN CALL YOU NAMES BUT DON'T CALL ME NAMES

Of obligations, by far the solemnest
Burden the conscientious columnist.
The world lies on his volcanic shoulders;
Sometimes he flames, sometimes just smoulders.
Each morn he expounds to me and you
Just what we ought to think and do,
Or explains to us, by the setting sun,
Exactly what we ought to have done.
Besides the citizens and the nation,
He has another obligation—
The syndicated right divine
To keep other columnists in line.
Then who can blame him for his temper
When people continue so *sic semper*?
So go it, Westbrook,
And go it, Drew,
Tally-ho, yoicks, and view halloo!

How the hide and the ivory fly about
When two bull columnists fall out!
One of them stepped on the other's feet,
He was eastbrook-bound on a westbrook street,
And, before you could say Louella Parsons,
There were libels and barratries, torts and arsons.
Only *The Times* continued to fiddle
While civilization split down the middle,

While kegler spat upon brother kegler,
Senior for Pearson, cadet for Pegler,
While millions of millions of plain pe-ople,
From Canada to Constantinople,
Held their breath, and followed each shot,
And wondered who would settle for what.

Then go it, Westbrook,
And go it, Drew,
Tally-ho, yoicks, and view halloo!
It's like when Stalin
Was feuding Hitler,
Just—excuse the expression—
A little bit littler.

CALLING SPRING VII–MMMC

As an old traveller, I am indebted to paper-bound thrillers,
Because you travel faster from Cleveland to Terre Haute when you travel with a lapful of victims and killers.
I am by now an authority on thumbprints and fingerprints and even kneeprints,
But there is one mystery I have never been able to solve in certain of my invaluable reprints.
I am happily agog over their funerals, which are always satisfactorily followed by exhumerals,
But I can't understand why so many of them carry their copyright lines in Roman numerals.
I am just as learned as can be,
But if I want to find out when a book was first published, I have to move my lips and count on my fingers to translate Copyright MCMXXXIII into Copyright 1933.
I have a horrid suspicion
That something lies behind the publisher's display of erudition.
I may be oversensitive to clues,
But I detect a desire to obfuscate and confuse.
Do they think that because a customer cannot translate MCMXXXIII into 1933 because he is not a classical scholar,
He will therefore assume the book to have been first published yesterday and will therefore sooner lay down his XXV cents or I/IV of a dollar?
Or do they, straying equally far from the straight and narrow,

Think that the scholarly will snatch it because the Roman copyright line misleads him to believe it the work of Q. Horatius Flaccus or P. Virgilius Maro?

Because anybody can make a mistake when dealing with MCMs and XLVs and things, even Jupiter, ruler of gods and men;

All the time he was going around with IO he pronounced it Ten.

EVERYBODY'S MIND TO ME A KINGDOM IS
or
A GREAT BIG WONDERFUL WORLD IT'S

Some melodies are popular as well as classical, which I suppose makes them popsicles,
And some poems are part William Cullen Bryant and part Nick Kenny which makes them thanatopsicles,
And to some people Wisconsin is what Guinevere was to Launcelot,
And if they are away from it they are Wisconsolate.
Some naturalists know why the sphinx is sphinxlike and the griffin is griffiny,
And some couples are so wealthy that even their tiffs are from Tiffany.
Some Angeleno socialites fine each other a dollar
If they say La Jolla,
And give each other a Picasso or a Goya
For pronouncing it La Hoya.
Why should not I pick up a masterpiece or a coin?
I will no longer say Des Moines,
I shall sail into the C. B. & Q. ticket office like a swan,
And ask for a lower to Day Mwahn.
This I shall do because I am a conscientious man, when I throw rocks at sea birds I leave no tern unstoned,
I am a meticulous man, and when I portray baboons I leave no stern untoned,
I am a man who values the fitness of things above notoriety and pelf,

Which is why I am happy I heard the cockney postmaster say to a doctor who was returning a leprechaun to Gloccamorra in an open envelope, Physician, seal thy h'elf.

NEXT!

I thought that I would like to see
The early world that used to be,
That mastodonic mausoleum,
The Natural History Museum.
Newspaper full of physicists,
I dropped my head upon my fists.
On iron seat in marble bower,
I slumbered through the closing hour.
At midnight in the vasty hall
The fossils gathered for a ball.
High above notices and bulletins
Loomed up the Mesozoic skeletons.
Aroused by who knows what elixirs,
They ground along like concrete mixers.
They bowed and scraped in reptile pleasure,
And then began to tread the measure.
There were no drums or saxophones,
But just the clatter of their bones,
A rolling, rattling carefree circus
Of mammoth polkas and mazurkas.
Pterodactyls and brontosauruses
Sang ghostly prehistoric choruses.
Amid the megalosauric wassail
I caught the eye of one small fossil.
Cheer up, old man, he said, and winked—
It's kind of fun to be extinct.

THEY WON'T BELIEVE, ON NEW YEAR'S EVE, THAT NEW YEAR'S DAY WILL COME WHAT MAY

How do I feel to-day? I feel as unfit as an unfiddle,
And it is the result of a certain turbulence in the mind
and an uncertain burbulence in the middle.
What was it anyway, that angry thing that flew at me?
I am unused to banshees crying Boo at me.
Your wife can't be a banshee,
Or can she?
Of course, some wives become less fond
When you're bottled in bond.
My Uncle George, in lavender-scented Aunt Edna's day,
If he had a glass of beer on Saturday night, he didn't
dare come home till the following Wednesday.
I see now that he had hit upon the ideal idea,
The passage of time, and plenty of it, is the only marital
panacea.
Ah, if the passage of time were backward, and last night
I'd been a child again, this morning I'd be fragrant
with orange-juice,
Instead of reeking of pinch-bottle foreign juice;
But if I should turn out to be a child again, what would
life hold for me?
The woman I love would be too old for me.
There's only one solution to my problem, a hair of the
dog, or maybe a couple of hairs;
Then if she doesn't get mad at me life will be peaceful,
and if she does, it will show she really cares.

CHANGE HERE FOR WICHITA FALLS
or
HAS ANYBODY SEEN MY WANDERLUST?

Luxury travel is something for which I pant;
But who can afford it? The Aga Khan, and I can't.
Would I had studied Oriental languages as a pup;
I am always going to places where the time-table says
Read UP.
Trains that me back to ole Virginny or ole Indianny
carry,
They have always just dropped off the diner at Harrisburg or Wilkes-Barre, which I always get confused
with John Wilkes-Barre.
Of streamliners and stratodomers I have heard gladsome
tidings,
But to me they are simply blinding streaks to make way
for which I have spent innumerable hours on rusty
sidings.
To some people travel conjures up a picture of
luggage plastered with glamorous labels and
tags;
To me it is a picture of a remote station platform with
no porters and taxis, just me and my sacroiliac and
three heavy bags.
I am told that the comforts in modern hotels are stunning;
My experience is that a hotel is a place with the elevator
out of order where you can only wash one hand
at a time because there is no stopper for the drain
and you have to keep squeezing the handles of the
faucet to keep the water running.

That is the hard way to get an ablution;
It reminds me of the visitor to the Chinese zoo who asked what language the aquatic carnivora talked, Pidgin English? and the keeper replied, No, Otter Confucian.

DON'T LOOK FOR THE SILVER LINING, JUST WAIT FOR IT

The rabbit loves his hoppity and the wallaby loves his
hippity.
I love my serendipity.
Let none look askance;
Serendipity is merely the knack of making happy and
unexpected discoveries by chance.
Only yesterday I was bored by a bore—there is no topic
that he isn't inept on it—
And when I pointed out a piece of chewing-gum on the
sidewalk, he was too busy talking to listen, so I
soon made the happy and unexpected discovery
that he had stepped on it.
It was serendipity when a recent hostess of mine
in Philadelphia apologized for serving ham
and eggs because she had forgotten to order
scrapple,
Just as it was when I found a bow tie I could
wear that didn't rise and fall with my Adam's
apple.
I called it happy and unexpected when I found a funny
paper with something funny in it,
And when I found a hole in my pocket but hadn't
lost any money because I didn't have any money
in it,
Also when I found a hole in my pocket which I had
tickets for a harp recital in, or in which I had
tickets for a harp recital, to put it properer,
So instead of the harp recital we had to see the Marx
Brothers in *A Night at the Opera.*

If your coat catches on a branch just as you are about to
slip over a precipice precipitous,
That's serendipitous,
But when you happily and unexpectedly discover that
you don't have to go to the dentist or the chiropo-
dist,
That's serendopitist.

POLONIUS, YES, POLONIUS, NO

I have always regretted that Hamlet slew Polonius,
With whom I think I would have got along very harmonious.
Polonius said: 'Neither a borrower nor a lender be,'
And that applies to me,
Because, as he continued: 'loan oft loseth both itself and friend,'
Which is grist for my mill, since I both have no credit to borrow on and no loans to lend.
However, Polonius also said: 'Costly thy habit as thy purse can buy,'
Which is surely a personal matter between the little tailor around the corner and I.
If I want to dress parsimonious,
What's that to Polonius?
My own rule of thumb is: 'Costly thy raiment
As the first payment,'
But even had I the gold of Ophir,
I'd still feel entitled to go around wearing one wedgie and one loafer.
Obviously Polonius was a busybody whom no snub could embarrass,
So on second thought I don't regret that Hamlet stabbed him behind the arras.

THE CATERPILLAR

I find among the poems of Schiller
No mention of the caterpillar,
Nor can I find one anywhere
In Petrarch or in Baudelaire,
So here I sit in extra session
To give my personal impression.
The caterpillar, as it's called,
Is often hairy, seldom bald;
It looks as if it never shaves;
When as it walks, it walks in waves;
And from the cradle to the chrysalis
It's utterly speechless, songless, whistleless.

THE TOUCAN

The toucan's profile is prognathous,
Its person is a thing of bathos.
If even I can tell a toucan
I'm reasonably sure that you can.

THE PLATYPUS

I like the duck-billed platypus
Because it is anomalous.
I like the way it raises its family,
Partly birdly, partly mammaly.
I like its independent attitude.
Let no one call it a duck-billed platitude.

THE HAMSTER

There is not much about the hamster
To stimulate the epigramster.
The essence of his simple story,
He populates the laboratory.
Then leaves his offspring in the lurch,
Martyrs to medical research.
Was he as bright as people am,
New York would be New Hamsterdam.

How often I've been overawed
By visiting lecturers from abroad,
Who glimpse our land in ten-day trips,
Between inbound and outbound ships,
Returning swiftly to their homes
To write encyclopaedic tomes
Condemning all, not overlooking
Our wives, our culture, and our cooking.

Of late, however, the foreign celebrity
Has yielded to native muliebrity,
By which ten-dollar phrase I mean
That lady lecturers stole the scene.
And how shall we distinguish, then,
The feminine speakers from the men?
The ladies have different architecture,
And make more money when they lecture.

But be they man or be they woman,
Lecturers have one trait in common;
For both the ladies and the gents
Seem to deplore their audience,
Wherefore they charge their hearers twice,
Their hearers pay a double price,
And double jeopardy they tote about;
First to be talked at, then to be wrote about.

How Fate on lecturers unleashes
Woes not unleashed on lesser species!

In return for money, plus expenses,
They suffer uncouth experi-ences.
What C.P.A. has come across
Raw oysters bathed in chocolate sauce?
What salesman roaming all the earth
Finds hedgehogs in his lower berth?

The greatest burden lecturers bear
Is meeting kindness everywhere.
Next year they black-list the locality
That shows the greatest hospitality,
For there is nothing that they hate
Like meeting those who pay the freight.
Successful ones insist their host
Shall treat them like the Holy Ghost.

Well, after this morose preamble,
I take a calculated gamble.
Remembering a recent trek
I venture to stick out my neck,
For I have hoisted on the platform
My tall, but in-the-middle-fat, form,
And purpose, if it please the court,
To file a minority report.

I do not claim, with ostentation,
That I have covered all the nation;
Still, for a freshman in the art,
I've made a reasonable start,
And lived in thirty-seven states
Through several hundred lecture dates.

Some people North and West and South
Don't know I ever close my mouth.

From Baltimore on the Chesapeake
I set out to speak and speak and speak.
I rode the Santa Fe and Pennsy,
And motored in S. C. and in N. C.,
And omnibused vertically, by gosh,
From Lewiston, I., to Pullman, Wash.
I learned that speaking brings on eczema,
And it's Yaki-ma, and not Ya-kima.

I've swallowed, in storms I near got lost in,
Dust in Texas and snow in Boston,
I've had waffle cookies in Fond du Lac,
And in Lincoln, a sacroiliac,
A token of Bryan's jealous wrath,
But I found an Omaha osteopath,
Thanks to whose ministrations fabulous
Neb. is to me no longer nebulous.

I've followed Northbound spring up hill
From Georgia to Jefferson's Charlottesville,
I've watched the garish Hollywood golfers,
And basketball at Gustavus Adolphus,
And on the shores of Puget Sound
The original theatre in the round;
And be it anomalous, or analamous,
I've enlightened the scientists at Los Alamos.

In Cleveland I've roamed Lake Erie's side,
Two full-fledged rabbis for my guide,
Baited professors without rebuke
Over a midnight-cap at Duke,
And in Florida, without a Collins,
Seen a president installed at Rollins.
I've seen the cypress and the yucca,
And a limestone statue of Joe Palooka.

Hardly among our current scarcities
Are colleges and universities;
So far I've visited ninety of them,
And, since they've been polite, I love them.
During the progress of my calls
On Quonset huts and ivied halls
I found no student and no dean
Resembling those upon the screen.

Colleges great and small I saw,
Chicago and Kent and Wichita,
North-western and northern Idaho,
Washington, Pittsburgh, New Mexico,
Everywhere kids and G.I.s together
Were chasing ideas, hell for leather.
Time has ploughed under dear old Siwash;
The freshwater college jape is eyewash.

The noses in dust I'd like to rub
Of those who jeer at the woman's club.

They seem to deem male joiners manly,
Like Hemingway, Livingstone, and Stanley,
But should the women form in groups,
It proves them pretentious nincompoops.
Yet between Spokane and Grand Rapids
I noted a dearth of female Babbitts.

The ladies accept the rap unheeding
And quietly keep up their reading.
The members as well as Madam Chairman
Know Christopher Fry from S. N. Behrman;
They know Brancusi from St Gaudens,
And Eliot's point of view from Auden's.
Some are even as handy with Greek and Latin
As any glamour girl in Manhattan.

I recently baulked when I was looking in
A book that the author derided their cooking in,
Whose every chapter was all adrip
With peanut butter and marshmallow whip.
Why, before and after intoning ballads
I ate steaks and turkeys and plain green salads,
And from Sacramento to Cincinnati
I never caught sight of a chicken patty.

There's lots of land between the oceans,
And lots of people with lots of notions,
They're rural, and urban, and suburban;
They drink coffee, or coke, or Scotch, or bourbon;
And every region is proud to preach
Its way of life and way of speech;

Every state is a separate star,
With its own approach to the letter R.

The Middle West is doing nice
And doesn't need the East's advice;
It reads the Colonel for his comics,
Not for his theories on atomics.
The South may consign the North to Sheol
For confusing you-all and thou-all or thee-all;
But it seemed to me, from where I stood,
Our relations with us were pretty good.

Kansans, New Englanders, Carolinians
Stick to their ornery own opinions;
People don't swallow political prattle
With the single-mindedness of cattle;
People in overalls or mink
Are smarter than politicians think;
There is still a God's plenty left in people
Of the little red school and the tall white steeple.

I do not claim to be an oracle,
I state no statements categorical,
I'm just saying thanks for what I found
While I was wandering around.
Humility is a wholesome victual,
But why shouldn't the eagle scream a little?
If we differ on Truman or vivisection
We can always wait for the next election.

That the Stork is New York and America Billingsley,
Is a party line I'd follow unwillingsley,

So here's a thought which could be worser,
If you're East, look West, and vice versa.
The piano stretches from seaboard to seaboard;
Strike all the notes upon the keyboard.
The harmony rises, eagle-flighted,
The United States are still united.

TWO GOES INTO TWO ONCE, IF YOU CAN GET IT THERE

All my life I have been a witness of things,
Among which I keep witnessing the eternal unfitness of things.
Daily it is my wont
To notice how things that were designed to fit each other, don't.
Getting a cigarette into a cigarette-holder is like the round hole and the square peg,
And getting the cork back into the vermouth bottle is like reinserting the cuckoo in the egg.
Why is the card-case always just a smidgin smaller than the deck?
Why does it take a 15¾ collar to encircle a 15½ neck?
Experience is indeed a teacher, and I have learned this fact from it,
That no suit-case is large enough to recontain the clothes you just unpacked from it.
No wonder the grapes set on edge the teeth of the little foxes;
The minute you buy a dozen silver or brocade or leather match-box holders the match-box makers change the size of the boxes.
I am baffled, I weave between Scylla and Charybdis, between a writ of replevin and a tort;
I shall console myself with the reflection that even in this world, ever perverse and ever shifting, two pints still make one cavort.

THE CHEF HAS IMAGINATION
or
IT'S TOO HARD TO DO IT EASY

Hark to a lettuce lover.
I consider lettuce a blessing.
And what do I want on my lettuce?
Simply a simple dressing.

But in dining-car and hostel
I grow apoplectic and dropsical;
Is this *dressing* upon my lettuce,
Or is it a melting popsicle?

A dressing is not the meal, dears,
It requires nor cream nor egg,
Nor butter nor maple sugar,
And neither the nut nor the meg.

A dressing is not a compote,
A dressing is not a custard;
It consists of pepper and salt,
Vinegar, oil, and mustard.

It is not paprika and pickles,
Let us leave those to the Teutons;
It is not a pinkish puddle
Of grenadine and Fig Newtons.

Must I journey to France for dressing?
It isn't a baffling problem;
Just omit the molasses and yoghurt,
The wheat germ, and the Pablum.

It's oil and vinegar, dears,
No need to tiddle and toil;
Just salt and pepper and mustard,
And vinegar, and oil.

For Brillat-Savarin, then, and Hoyle,
Stick, friends, to vinegar and oil!
Yachtsman, jettison boom and spinnaker,
Bring me oil and bring me vinegar!
Play the music of Haydn or Honegger,
But lace it with honest oil and vinegar!
Choir in church or mosque or synagogue,
Sing, please, in praise of oil and vinegogue.
I'm not an expert, just a beginneger,
But I place my trust in oil and vinegar.
May they perish, as Remus was perished by Romulus,
Who monkey with this, the most sacred of formulas.

WHY THE POSTMAN HAS TO RING TWICE
or
YELLOW ENVELOPE, WHERE HAVE YOU GONE?

Captain Ahab's desire was the White Whale.
My desire is to receive a telegram by telegraph messenger and not by telephone or mail.
If I should be asked, What hath God wrought? by Samuel F. B. Morse's ghost,
I should reply, He hath wrought the Telephone Company and the United States Post,
And I am still trying to read the riddle
Of how the Telegraph Company got that cosy seat in the middle.
Oh Company uncertain, coy, and hard to please,
In the unprogressive olden times they relied on reliable elderly boys with bicycles and puttees,
But now a telegram seems to be something that if they can't mail it or phone it,
They disown it.
You stand convicted of impudence and effrontry
If you wish a telegram delivered, not mailed, to a person without a telephone in either the city or, what they never heard of, the country.
Do not try to appease me, I am unappeasable,
For every time I send an important telegram to be personally delivered I am inevitably notified just too late next day that delivery was impractical and unfeasible.

Telegraph Company, you are the darling of my heart,
    I adore you,
In token of which I present you with a new slogan:
    Don't write, telegraph; we will mail it for you.

THE WILD JACKASS

Have ever you harked to the jackass wild,
Which scientists call the onager?
It sounds like the laugh of an idiot child,
Or a hepcat on a harmoniger.
But do not sneer at the jackass wild,
There is method in his hee-haw,
For with maidenly blush and accent mild
The jenny-ass answers, shee-haw.

THE TORTOISE

Come crown my brows with leaves of myrtle;
I know the tortoise is a turtle.
Come carve my name in stone immortal;
I know the turtoise is a tortle;
I know to my profound despair;
I bet on one to beat a hare.
I also know I'm now a pauper
Because of its tortley turtley torpor.

THE AQUARIUM

Some fish are minnows,
Some are whales.
People like dimples,
Fish like scales.
Some fish are slim,
And some are round.
Fish don't get cold,
And don't get drowned.
But every fish wife
Is jealous for her fish
Of what we call mermaids,
And they call merfish.

THE MULES

In the world of mules
There are no rules.

THE CUCKOO

Cuckoos lead Bohemian lives,
They fail as husbands and as wives,
Therefore they cynically disparage
Everybody else's marriage.

THE BIRDS

Puccini was Latin, and Wagner Teutonic,
And birds are incurably philharmonic.
Suburban yards and rural vistas
Are filled with avian Andrews Sisters.
The skylark sings a roundelay,
The crow sings 'The Road to Mandalay,'
The nightingale sings a lullaby
And the sea-gull sings a gullaby.
That's what shepherds listened to in Arcadia
Before sombody invented the radia.

THE SWAN

Scholars call the masculine swan a cob;
I call him a narcissistic snob.
He looks in the mirror over and over,
And claims to have never heard of Pavlova.

THE VOLUBLE WHEEL-CHAIR

When you roll along admiring the view,
And everyone drives too fast but you;
When people not only ignore your advice,
But complain that you've given it to them twice;
When you babble of putts you nearly holed,
By gad, sir,
You are getting old.

When for novels you lose your appetite
Because writers don't write what they used to write;
When by current art you are unbeguiled,
And pronounce it the work of an idiot child;
When cacophonous music leaves you cold,
By gad, sir,
You are getting old.

When you twist the sheets from night to morn
To recall when a cousin's daughter was born;
When youngsters mumble and won't speak up,
And your dog dodders, who was a pup;
When the modern girl seems a hussy bold,
By gad, sir,
You are getting old.

When you scoff at feminine fashion trends;
When strangers resemble absent friends;
When you start forgetting the neighbours' names
And remembering bygone football games;
When you only drop in at the club to scold,
By gad, sir,
You are getting old.

But when you roar at the income tax,
And the slippery bureaucratic hacks,
And the ancient political fishlike smell,
And assert that the world is going to hell,
Why you are not old at all, at all;
By gad, sir,
You are on the ball.

THE CHILD IS FATHER TO THE MAN, BUT WITH MORE AUTHORITY

Once there were some children and they were uninterested in chores,
And they never picked anything up or put anything back or brought anything in from out of doors.
They didn't want to take care of anything, just to play with it,
And their parents let them get away with it.
Little did they know that Nemesis
Was on the premises.
Their regrets were at first scant
When they were left alone on their island summer home because their parents were called away by the convalescence of a wealthy aunt.
They prepared to take advantage of nobody being around,
And this is what they found,
This is how they were hoist with their own petards,
There wasn't a deck with more than fifty-one cards,
And when they tried to play the handsome phonograph with which they were equipped,
The records were either lost, warped, or chipped,
There were bows but no arrows, and bats and gloves but no ball,
And the untethered rowboat had drifted beyond recall,
And when they were wet the only towels were those strewn on the bathroom floor where moisture lingers,

And when they were cold they couldn't light a fire because all the matches had been used by people seeing how far down they would burn without burning their fingers.

Such experiences certainly taught them a lesson, and when their parents returned to their native heath,

Why, the first thing these children did was to leave the window open so it rained in on the piano, and go to bed without brushing their teeth.

THE VISIT

She welcomes him with pretty impatience
And a cry of Greetings and salutations!
To which remark, no laggard, he
Ripostes with a Long time no see.
Recovering her poise full soon,
She bids him Anyhoo, sit ye doon,
And settling by the fireside,
He chuckles, Thank you, kind sir, she cried.
Snug as a bug, the cup he waits
That cheers but not inebriates.
She offers him a truly ducal tea,
Whipped up, she says, with no diffewclty.
A miracle, if I didn't know you,
He says—It only shows to go you.
Eying her o'er the fragrant brew,
He tells her her smile is picturescue,
And now he whispers, a bit pajamaly,
That he's fed to the teeth with his whole fam damily,
Perhaps she'll forgive an old man's crotchet
And visit Bermuda on his yachat.
She says she might, despite Dame Rumour,
Because he is a who than whom none is whomer.
He sidles close, but no cigar—
Until the yachat, au reservoir.

A DOG'S BEST FRIEND IS HIS ILLITERACY

It has been well said that quietness is what a Grecian urn is the still unravished bride of,
And that a door is what a dog is perpetually on the wrong side of.
I may add that a sachet is what many a housewife's linen is fragrantly entrusted to,
But that a cliché is what a dog owner must eventually get adjusted to.
Whether your visitor be Mr Belvedere or Bennett Cerf, what does he say when your dog greets him with Southern hospitality and salutes him all kissin'-cousiny?
He says: 'He smells my dog on me, doesn't he?'
And he asks: 'How old is he?' and you say 'Twelve,' and he appraises Spot with the eye of an antiquarian,
And says: 'Seven twelves are eighty something, why Spot in human terms you 're an octogenarian,'
But these two bromides are just the rattle before the strike,
Because then he says it 's funny but he 's noticed how often dogs and their masters look alike.
Such are the comments faced by dog owners from Peoria to Peshawar,
And frequently from a man who in canine terms is 322 years old, and he is the spit and image of his own Chihuahua.

The only escape is to have something instead of dogs but whatever I substituted I should probably err,
And if I ended up with raccoons every guest would turn out to be a raccoonteur.

WE PAUSE NOW BRIEFLY FOR AN IMPORTANT MESSAGE

To be grateful for small favours I am nothing loath,
Wherefore I have been recently counting my blessings, employing for the purpose the fingers of a three-toed sloth.
Blessing number one, although to appreciate it I am dilatory,
Is that as a child I was dropped chin-first into a barrel of depilatory,
So, not being that one man in seven who must shave every day, guess what I have never owned:
The precision razor equipped zip-twist with the sharpest edges ever honed.
I could never afford to own such a razor, because on T.V. I have seen with my own eyes that modern technology has made it so precise
That if you drop it once it gets all out of line and you can't use it twice,
You have to go out and buy a new precision razor right away,
And I know that between my tic and my palsy I would be in the market for a new precision razor at least every other day.
Blessing number two is that I didn't achieve my ambition to play for the Yankees or the Dodgers or the Giants
At least not since salesmanship has become a science.
Because think how it must add to a patriotic ball-player's normal humiliation and regrets

To know that every time he doesn't complete a double play or hit a home run some Veterans' Hospital is deprived of six hundred less-irritating cigarettes.
Blessing number three is that though my head is now considerably smaller than my waist
At least an advertising man is something I am not so stupid as and as which I haven't got as bad taste.

EHEU! FUGACES
or
WHAT A DIFFERENCE A LOT OF DAYS MAKE

When I was seventeen or so,
I scoffed at money-grubbers.
I had a cold contempt for dough,
And I wouldn't wear my rubbers.
No aspirin I took for pains,
For pests no citronella,
And in the Aprilest of rains
I carried no umbrella.

When I was young I was Sidney Carton,
Proudly clad in a Spartan tartan.
To-day I'd be, if I were able,
Just healthy, wealthy, and comfortable.

When I was young I would not yield
To comforters and bed socks,
In dreams I covered centre field
For the Giants or the Red Sox.
I wished to wander hence and thence,
From diamond mine to gold field,
Or piloting a Blitzen Benz,
Outdistance Barney Oldfield.

When I subscribed to *The Youth's Companion*
I longed to become a second D'Artagnan.
To-day I desire a more modest label:
He's healthy, wealthy, and comfortable.

When I was pushing seventeen,
I hoped to bag a Saracen;
To-day should one invade the scene,
I'd simply find it embaracen.
Ah, Postumus, no wild duck I,
But just a waddling puddle duck,
So here's farewell to the open sky
From a middle-aged fuddy-duddle duck.

When I was young I was Roland and Oliver,
Nathan Hale and Simón Bolívar.
To-day I would rather side-step trouble,
And be healthy, wealthy, and comfortuble.

EVERYBODY WANTS TO GET INTO THE BAEDEKER

Most travellers eavesdrop
As unintentionally as autumn leaves drop,
Which brings up a question that confronts every conscientious traveller:
Should he, or should he not, of overheard misinformation be an unraveller?
The dear little old lady in front of you asks, What river is that, is it the Swanee or the Savannah?
And somebody who has no idea firmly says, It 's the Potomac. It happens to be the Susquehanna.
The visiting Englishman asks, What is that mountain, and somebody yells, Pike's Peak! into his ear.
It isn't. It 's Mt Rainier.
Can one oneself of responsibility disembarrass
When one hears a fellow passenger being assured that the *Île de France* sails right up the Seine to Paris?
What is the etiquette
When one hears an eager sightseer being informed that Greenwich Village is in Connecticut?
It is my experience that people who volunteer information are people who don't know the Eiffel Tower from the Tower of Pisa,
Or Desdemona from the Mona Lisa.
I am convinced that they have learned their geography through drawing moustaches on girls on travel posters,
And have done their own travelling exclusively on roller coasters.

What is that, madam? How do you get from 42nd
Street and Broadway to Times Square?
Sorry, madam, but it's impossible to get from here to
there.

OLD DR VALENTINE TO HIS ONLY MILLIONAIRE

I remember the shape you were in when you went
From the ambulance into the oxygen tent.
Your kidneys were clogged, your liver was leather;
I took you apart, then put you together.
I hear that to-day you're a Sedgman at tennis,
A Hogan at golf, and an amorous menace.
There's only one effort too much for you still:
To pick up your pen and pay my bill.

OLD DR VALENTINE TO THAT KIND OF PATIENT

During office hours I'm agog for your question,
Is it your heart, or indigestion?
But after your evening alcoholic
Of rye and champagne and lobster and garlic
When you phone me and wake me, I tell you flatly,
Please reverse the charges and call Clement Attlee.

OLD DR VALENTINE TO A COLLEAGUE

I have a patient's mother
Who hovers over me
And everything that I prescribe
That mother's bound to see.
She's read the Sunday papers
So she knows a hundred cures,
She knows more medicine than I,
And, Doctor, she is yours!

OLD DR VALENTINE TO HIS SON

Your hopeless patients will live,
Your healthy patients will die.
I have only this word to give:
Wonder, and find out why.

OLD DR VALENTINE FOR ONCE DREAMS OF WEALTH

Dr Valentine hopes to announce
He's collecting fantastic amounts.
He's invented a bra
Called Peps-oo-la-la
Which delivers more bounce to the ounce.

ROLL OVER AND PLAY ALIVE

or

WHO SAYS YOU CAN'T TEACH AN OLD DOG TIRESOME TRICKS?

Brooks are often called rippling, but rivers are really ripplinger,
And some writers are called Kipling when others are Kiplinger,
And I understand that there was a turn-of-the-century joke by which Mr Kipling's surface was really rippled:
Algernon: Do you like Kipling? *Sweet Young Thing*: I don't know, I 've never kippled.
I like making jokes, too,
But often it 's so hard to make up my own that I take a tip from radio and employ the switcheroo.
For years I led the conversation around to Missouri until people got trapped into asking me how I liked Joplin, and my, how their faces toppled
When I told them I had never joppled.
Now, alas, I must say farewell to my hardy-perennial joke and pack it away in lavender and old poplin,
I have just been to, and been delighted with, Joplin,
And I have different ethics from a propagandizing Slav,
So how can I henceforth claim never to have joppled when I really and truly have?
Which way to turn? I can as well imagine Southern California agentless, or Little America snowless,
As me *bon mot*-less.
But hark, I hear the bugles of the switcheroo!
What works one time might as well work two.

I will imagine a jolly, untravelled Irish spinster,
One who has never seen either the Blarney Stone or
Westminster,
And her friends Yeats and Synge and Lady Gregory,
to make it a really name-worthy anecdote, ask her
how she likes Dublin, and what does she say?
Well, the payoff follows as the night the day.

THE WENDIGO *

The Wendigo,
The Wendigo!
Its eyes are ice and indigo!
Its blood is rank and yellowish!
Its voice is hoarse and bellowish!
Its tentacles are slithery,
And scummy,
Slimy,
Leathery!
Its lips are hungry blubbery,
And smacky,
Sucky,
Rubbery!
The Wendigo,
The Wendigo!
I saw it just a friend ago!
Last night it lurked in Canada;
To-night, on your veranada!
As you are lolling hammockwise
It contemplates you stomachwise.
You loll,
It contemplates,
It lollops.
The rest is merely gulps and gollops.

* *Wendigo*: In the mythology of the northern Algonquians, an evil spirit; one of a fabulous tribe of cannibals.

Webster's Unabridged Dictionary.

MR BETTS'S MIND A KINGDOM IS

Do you know my friend Mr Betts?
He claims he forgets.
When urged by Mrs Betts to tell you about their trip to California he says he has no memory,
He is in a dilemma, he looks dilemmary.
He looks like a high-school music teacher substituting at the last minute for Iturbi,
And then he gives you a precise blow by blow, palm-tree by palm-tree, movie star by movie star account, starting at the Grand Central and finishing with an appreciation of the waitresses' rear elevation at the Brown Derby.
My friend Mr Betts
Claims he forgets.
When asked by Mrs Betts to tell you about that radio programme that made her laugh, she thought she 'd smother,
He says everything goes in one ear and out the other,
After which he takes the floor like Winston Churchill,
And re-creates the entire half hour from the first joke about the ungainly spinster who can't get a man to the final commerchill.

Do you know my friend Mr Betts?
I wish I could remember as accurately as he forgets.

THE STRANGE CASE OF THE CAUTIOUS MOTORIST

Have you read the biography of Mr Schwellenbach?
You can miss it if you try.
Mr Schwellenbach didn't have much to live for, but he didn't want to die.
Therefore he was not only cautious, he was timid,
And if a savage-looking panhandler said to him, Gimme, he didn't call up the Better Business Bureau, he just gimmied.
Statistics of automobile fatalities filled his brain,
And he never drove over 25 miles an hour, and always, I regret to say, in the right-hand lane.
Whenever he stopped for a red light he cut off the ignition, put on the hand brake, locked all the doors, checked his licence and registration cards, and looked in the glove compartment to see if he had mice,
So when the light turned green everybody behind him had to wait while he de-moused the car, reassured himself that he was driving legally, unlocked the doors, released the hand brake, reignited the ignition, pressed the wrong button and turned on Bing Crosby instead of the motor, and the light turned from green to red to green thrice.
Every autumn with the rains
Mr Schwellenbach bought a new pair of chains.
He kept a record of every lethal blowout in the Western Hemisphere since 1921 in his files,
And he turned in his tyres for new ones every 750 miles.

Well, he was driving on his new tyres at 25 miles an hour in the right-hand lane of a dual highway last week, was Mr Schwellenbach,

And a car coming the other way owned by a loan shark who had bought his old tyres cheap had a blowout and jumped the dividing line and knocked him to hellenbach.

THE UNWINGED ONES

I don't travel on planes.
I travel on trains.
Once in a while, on trains,
I see people who travel on planes.
Every once in a while I'm surrounded
By people whose planes have been grounded.
I'm enthralled by their air-minded snobbery,
Their exclusive hobnobbery,
And I'll swear to, before any notary,
The clichés of their coterie.
They feel that they have to explain
How they happen to be on a train,
For even in Drawing Room A
They seem to feel *déclassé.*
So they sit with portentous faces
Clutching their attaché cases.
As the Scotches they rapidly drain
That they couldn't have got on the plane,
They grumble and fume about how
They'd have been in Miami by now.
They frowningly glance at their watches,
And order more Scotches.
By the time that they're passing through Rahway
They should be in Havana or Norway,
And they strongly imply that perhaps,
Since they're late, the world will collapse.
Then, as station merges with station,
They complain of the noise and vibration.
These outcasts of aviation,
They complain of the noise and vibration.

Sometimes on the train I'm surrounded
By people whose planes have been grounded.
That's the only trouble with trains;
When it fogs, when it smogs, when it rains,
You get people from planes.

WHAT IS BIBBIDI-BOBBIDI-BOO IN SANSKRIT?

When people tell me French is difficult, I show my dimple.
French is simple.
My pen is cosmopolitan, not parochial.
I am at home in French either classical or collochial.
I can pronounce *filet mignon* even while chewing it,
And I can and will fluently translate popular songs such as 'Everybody's doing it.'
Tout le monde est faisant le, faisant le, faisant le,
Tout le monde est faisant le,
Faisant quoi?
Dindon pas!
Vois ce ragtime couple débonnaire,
Vois-les jeter leurs épaules en air,
C'est un hibou,
Un hibou, un hibou,
Où?
I think that even Mr Berlin would agree that this has life and movement,
And that the few changes are an improvement.
That ragtime couple, for example, instead of just being vaguely over there,
They are now obviously in some expensive club, they are debonair.
And the substitution of *c'est un hibou, un hibou, un hibou* (it's an owl, it's an owl, it's an owl) for *c'est un ours, c'est un ours, c'est un ours* (it's a bear, it's a bear, it's a bear)—
That is a veritable *coup de tonnerre,*

'hat is a truly superior brand of merchandise,
ecause in French *ours* (bear) might be confused with
oursin (sea-urchin) and what would a debonair
owl-loving ragtime couple want with a fishy batch
of sea-urchindise?
feel I have built myself a monument of more than
bricks and mortar,
nd, having gained the gratitude of Mr Berlin, I am
now leafing through the works of Mr Oscar Hammerstein and Mr Cole Porter.

YOU CAN BE A REPUBLICAN, I'M A GERONTOCRAT

Oh, 'rorty' was a mid-Victorian word
Which meant 'fine, splendid, jolly,'
And often to me it has reoccurred
In moments melancholy.
For instance, children, I think it rorty
To be with people over forty.

I can't say which, come eventide,
More tedious I find;
Competing with the juvenile stride,
Or meeting the juvenile mind.
So I think it rorty, yes, and nifty,
To be with people over fifty.

The pidgin talk the youthful use
By-passes conversation.
I can't believe the code they choose
Is a means of communication.
Oh to be with people over sixty
Despite their tendency to prolixty!

The hours a working parent keeps
Mean less than Latin to them,
Wherefore they disappear in jeeps
Till three and four a.m.
Oh, to be with people you pour a cup for
Instead of people you have to wait up for!

I've tried to read young mumbling lips
Till I've developed a slant-eye,
But all I can read, between the quips,
Is, if I can't, why can't I?
Oh, to be beside a septuagenarian,
Silent upon a peak in Darien!

They don't know Hagen from Bobby Jones,
They never heard Al Smith,
Even Red Grange is beyond their range,
And Dempsey is a myth.
Oh golly, to gabble upon the shoulder
Of someone my own age, or even older!

I'm tired of defining hadn't oughts
To opposition mulish,
The thoughts of youth are long long thoughts,
And Jingo! Aren't they foolish!
All which is why, in case you've wondered
I'd like a companion aged one hundred.

CHLOE AND THE ROUÉ

When Lord Byron wrote so glowingly of the isles o
Greece
It was not mere coincidence or caprice.
Knowing his character and his environment,
I think we can guess what Lord Byron meant.
Nobody than Lord Byron could have been sorrier
About the death of a heroic Grecian warrior,
But nobody after so short a period
Could find consolation in the company of a nymph o
a Nereid,
So all praise to the nymphs of the isles of Greece.
May their tribe increase.
But their tribe won't increase if they all behave like
nymph named Chloe,
Who lived on the southernmost isle of Greece where i
is swampy, not snowy.
Chloe caught the attention of Zeus,
And he slipped away from the banquet hall mumblin
some ridiculous excuse,
And when Hera called after him to come back, sh
knew what it meant when he got all skittish an
scampery,
He said he'd be back for breakfast, he just had to se
a mortal about a lamprey,
And he didn't want to tell a lie so he disguised himsel
as a lamprey fisherman but he couldn't find hi
lamprey-fishing clothes,
So aside from his lamprey-spear he was as naked as a
narcissus or a rose,

and he tracked Chloe through the swamp and offered her his heart and a golden chariot, a dandy four-wheeler,
but she refused because she was a Southern nymph, a Hellenic Dixiecrat, and she had been taught never to trust a nude eeler.

Some people think the nose of the Sphinx was flattene
by Napoleon's cannoneers,
But it wasn't, not by several thousand years.
Credit should go to a person who dressed like Adam an
talked like Pericles,
This person being known to us as Hercules and to th
illiterate Greeks as Heracles,
And Hercules performed twelve fabulous labours,
Which caused all the inhabitants of Ultima Thule t
exclaim Begorra and Bejabers,
And just when he thought he was through with labour
he was told by the gods, several of whom were hi
cousin,
That he must make it a baker's dozen.
They said that all brawn and no brain makes a dul
demigod, so on immortality it was no dice
Unless he stumped the Sphinx thrice,
And Hercules said: Well I'll be a duck-billed platypus
Here is a chance to avenge my friend Oedipus,
And he assumed an expression deceptively pleasant,
And he asked the Sphinx: Who is the heavyweigh
champion? and she said: Ezzard Charles, and h
said: No it ezzant,
And he said: I'll give you another bone to pick at,
Why did Orpheus give up conducting and throw awa
his baton? and she said: I bet you don't know
either, and he said: Because there were mor
Bacchantes than he could shake a stick at,
And the Sphinx said: You can't stump me three times i
a row, and he said: A house full, a hole full, yo

cannot catch a bowlful, can you riddle me that
without straining?
nd she said: Smoke? and Hercules said: No thank you,
I 'm in training.
rom that point
he Sphinx's nose has been out of joint.

Once there was a Greek divinity of the sea named Ceto and she married a man named Phorcus,
And the marriage must have been pretty raucous;
Their remarks about which child took after which parent must have been full of asperities,
Because they were the parents of the Gorgons, and the Graeae, and Scylla, and the dragon that guarded the apples of the Hesperides.
Bad blood somewhere.
To-day the Gorgons are our topic, and as all schoolboys including you and me know,
They were three horrid sisters named Medusa and Euryale and Stheno,
But what most schoolboys don't know because they never get beyond their Silas Marners and their Hiawathas,
The Gorgons were not only monsters, they were also highly talented authors.
Medusa began it;
She wrote *Forever Granite*.
But soon Stheno and Euryale were writing, too, and they addressed her in daily choruses,
Saying we are three literary sisters just like the Brontës so instead of Gorgons why can't we be brontë-sauruses?
Well, Medusa may have been mythical but she wasn't mystical,
She was selfish and egotistical.
She saw wider vistas
Than simply being the sister of her sisters.

She replied, tossing away a petrified Argonaut on whom
she had chipped a molar,

You two can be what you like, but since I am the big
fromage in this family, I prefer to think of myself
as the Gorgon Zola.

LEDA'S FORTUNATE GAFFE

The Greeks called the king of the gods Zeus and th
Romans called him Jupiter.
Not that the Romans were stupider,
Jupiter being Roman for Zeus Pater, or Zeus th
Father,
Which was appropriate, rather.
Zeus Pater is not to be confused with Walter Pater,
Who flourished later.
I don't even know if Walter Pater had a wife,
But I bet he never poured into a lady's room disguise
as a shower of gold in his life.
Zeus Pater, on the other hand, was so eager to escap
the restraint of his jealous queen that once h
nearly killed a guard,
And in order to forward his unsavoury amours he im
personated just about everybody except Hilde
garde.
One day he tiptoed out through heaven's portal
And picked up the handkerchief of a succulent mortal,
But when he wished to continue the acquaintance, h
had run out of impersonations, he had nothing ne
to go as.
Juno always recognized him and followed him lik
Ruth after Boaz.
But this mortal happened to be Leda
And she was a great reader,
And when they were the equivalent of introduced,
Instead of Zeus, she thought the name was Proust,

And hey, hey!

The perplexing problem of what to impersonate was solved when she told him how much she admired *Swann's Way*.

HI-HO THE AMBULANCE-O

People on wheels hate people on feet,
It takes two to make a one-way street.
Traffic commissions plan and study,
And nearly every is a body.

BABY, IT'S CALDER INSIDE

In addition to beauty and utility
The genuine mobile has mobility.
You know it's art when assorted metals
Caress your brow like falling petals.

EVERYTHING'S HAGGIS IN HOBOKEN
or
SCOTS WHA HAE HAE

That hero my allegiance earns
Who boldly speaks of Robert Burns.
I have an inexpensive hobby—
Simply not to call him Bobbie.
It's really just as easy as not
Referring to Sir Wally Scott,
But many, otherwise resolute,
When mentioning Burns go coy and cute.
Scholars hip-deep in Homer and Horace
Suddenly turn all doch-an-dorris;
Fine ladies who should pose and purr
Roll out a half-rolled Highland burr;
Conventioneers in littered lobby
Hoist their glasses in praise of Bobbie;
All, all Burns-happy and Bobbie-loopy,
They dandle him like a Scotian kewpie.
I'll brush away like gnats and midges
Those who quote from Bobbies Southey and Bridges;
I will not snap my Hopalong gun
At admirers of Bobbie Stevenson
(To be Bobbied is no worse, I guess,
Than being enshrined as R.L.S.);
I'd even attempt to save from drowning
Maidens who dream of Bobbie Browning;
Who refers to Bobbie Rossellini
Is just a harmless betwixt-and-betweenie;
I try to withhold my acid formic
From readers of Colonel Bobbie McCormick;

And I would not sink my knife to the haft
In supporters of Senator Bobbie Taft.
But of Robert Burns I'm a serious fan,
He wrote like an angel and lived like a man,
And I yearn to shatter a set of crockery
On this condescending Bobbie-sockery.
Well, I 'm off, before I break the law,
To read Tommy Hardy and Bernie Shaw.

FATHER, DEAR FATHER, GO JUMP IN THE LAKE
or
YOU'RE COSTLIER THAN YOU THINK

Once there was a man named Mr Arents,
And he was the severest of parents.
Every time his seven children asked him when they could have a convertible he answered, by and by,
And he confiscated all their phonograph records that had songs with people singing, Aye yi aye yi.
He complained that they smoked too many cigarettes,
And he would neither feed nor bathe their pets.
He insulted all their friends at 4 a.m.
By standing at the head of the stairs in his pyjamas and remarking: Ahem.
He insisted that they put on their shoes before they ate,
And objected when they scooped the middles out of the rolls and deposited the crust on their plate.
That was the erstwhile Mr Arents,
The most unreasonable of parents.
You ought to see the new Mr Arents,
He is a veritable model of forbearance.
He feels that whatever his seven children request,
It behooves him to behave at their behest.
Mr Arents has had a warning,
Wherefore he brings them seven apples and seven convertibles each morning;
He is currying favour
Against the day his voice begins to quaver;

Any goodwill that his children may bear him, he wants to pad it,
He wants them to remember him as a right guy when he had it.
He knows that he is now an asset but he fears that all too soon
He will be an elderly liability in a chimney corner slurping porridge from a wooden spoon.
Mr Arents has recently been told by an annuity salesman something that makes him feel so singular that he has shrunk to Mr Arent:
Namely, it is easier for one parent to support seven children than for seven children to support one parent.

FATHER-IN-LAW OF THE GROOM

Our times will be in books interred
As the era of the eaten word,
So tell me why should I alone
By unprepared to eat my own?
The longer I live the sooner I find
How priceless is an open mind.
I trust that I am wiser plenty
At forty-nine than at nine and twenty.

How odd to think that once I rose
To sass my daughter's future beaux;
A new-born father, with arms akimbo,
Consigning all young men to limbo.
Since then I 've lived a fifth of a century
Incredibly charming and adventury,
As you would have, were your vicinity
One of exclusive femininity.

For years I saw no male but me;
Even our Bedlington was a she.
I stood apart and watched agog
My wife, my daughter, and my dog.
They are a higher form of life,
My dog, my daughter, and my wife,
Inhabitants of a fourth dimension
Too mystic for my comprehension.

Life was a song in ancient Greece,
No debutantes disturbed the peace,
No sirens moaning o'er their hair
Left Mr Paul for Mr Pierre,

And ladies conscious of their backs
Avoided blue jeans, shorts, and slacks,
Yet alone among women, even Achilles
Got heebie jeebies and the willies.

Therefore I hail this happy anomaly,
A fellow male within the family,
And cause my daughter's wrath to bloom
By monopolizing of her groom.
Oh, let the girls get on with the trousseau
Here's a man Friday at last for Crusoe,
To chew the fat and exchange the dope with,
And a simple masculine mind to cope with.

A girl and her words are equally random,
No use to attempt to understand 'em.
You behold in me a crafty vet
Of Hoover's day and I'm trying yet.
But Johnny's talk is a green oasis
Of presidential and pennant races;
His forthright speech my mind relaxes
Even when discussing taxes.

Linell, though I can't read you clearly
You know I love you long and dearly.
You know I wish you barrel on barrel
Of joy and health and fine apparel,
And clinking corpulent piggy banks,
And please to accept my heartfelt thanks
For bringing me, my angel chile,
A man to talk to once in a while.

WHAT'S IN A NAME? SOME LETTER I ALWAYS FORGET

Not only can I not remember anecdotes that are racy,
But I also can't remember whether the names of my Scottish friends begin with M-c or M-a-c,
And I can't speak for you, but for myself there is one dilemma with me in the middle of it,
Which is, is it Katharine with a K or Catherine with a C, and furthermore is it an A or is it an E in the middle of it?
I can remember the races between Man o' War and Sir Barton, and Épinard and Zev,
But I can't remember whether it's Johnson or Johnston any more than whether you address a minister as Mr or Dr or simply Rev.
I know a cygnet from a gosling and a coney from a leveret,
But how to distinguish an I-double-T from an E-double-T Everett?
I am familiar with the nature of an oath,
But I get confused between the Eliot with one L and one T, and the Elliot with two L's and one T, and the Eliott with one L and two T's, and the Elliott with two of both.
How many of my friendships have lapsed because of an extra T or a missing L;
Give me a simple name like Taliaferro or Wambsganss or Toporcer or Joralemon or Mankiewicz that any schoolboy can spell,

Because many former friends thought I was being im
polite to them
When it was only because I couldn't remember whethe
they were Stuarts with a U or Stewarts with an E-W
that I didn't write to them.

MERRY CHRISTMAS, YOU-ALL
or
WHO FORGOT SAVANNAH?

The men who draws the Christmas cards, dear,
They must have igloos in their yards, dear.
They lives in Labrador or Maine, dear.
They all knows how to harness reindeer.
They puts on snow-shoes and galoshes,
And breaks the ice before they washes.

The men who writes the Christmas rhymes,
They all inhabits frigid climes.
Their roofs is fluffy, I have heared,
With snow like Santa Claus's beard.
Icicles decorate their nose,
And chilblains nips their mistletoes.

I loves the artists and the bards
Who makes the pretty Christmas cards,
I loves their winter scenes and such,
But still I thinks they don't know much,
For Christmas wanders back and forth
And travels south as well as north.

I'm glad our Christmas sun arises.
On buttercups and butterflieses,
Our Christmas carol sounds as sweet
As if our ears was raw with sleet,
Our hearts is gay with Christmas mirth
Like on the colder parts of earth,
So cross the Mason-Dixon Line
And be my Christmas Valentine.

THE STRANGE CASE OF MR O'BANION'S COME-UPPANCE

Once there was a man named Mr O'Banion,
And he was a depressing companion.
He was so cynical
That it was practically clinical.
He was also a sceptic,
And would never eat a hamburger without first immersing it in antiseptic.
He believed that actresses exist on amours and marijuana,
And that St George's dragon was really a large iguana.
He stated that every man has his price,
And he was sure that bartenders use the same olive twice.
He was especially derisive of the names of summer cottages,
He said they stuck in his craws, of which he had developed two, and in his epiglottages.
He said there was nothing more fraudulent than a summer cottage's cognomen,
And one day he pointed out to his Scout troop that there were three large opaque billboards between Seaview Villa and the ocean, and that everybody was restless at Dunroamin.
He hinted that at Lilac Lodge you couldn't even raise dandelions, and scoffed that Mon Repos and Beau

Sejour would be the last place to find a French menu in,
And just as he remarked that Stuffed Sea Gull would be an apter name for Eagle's Eyrie, he was carried off by an eagle, and it was genuine.

HAND ME DOWN MY OLD SCHOOL SLIDING PADS

or

THERE'S A HINT OF STRAWBERRY LEAVES IN THE AIR

This is the outstretched, tentative toe,
The placid paddling into dotage:
To complement the radio
With the library of a summer cottage.

What calmer joy can life afford,
What more can fortune offer, or fame,
Than reading Mrs Humphry Ward
While listening to the baseball game?

A glimpse of ducal silhouettes,
A flash of electronic science,
As kind hearts clash with coronets—
Also the Cardinals with the Giants.

The heroine's birth is most unusual—
It's three and two on Enos Slaughter.
What would she think of Stanley Musial,
And he of Lady Rose's daughter?

The code of stout King Edward's reign
Conceals outstanding hanky-panky,
Suggesting time and time again
The hidden ball of Eddie Stanky.

Beware, fair child of Lady Rose;
Warkworth, that cad, is far too cuddly!
Ah! Sure as Bobby Thomson's throws,
She's rescued by the Duke of Chudleigh!

In a world where even umpires err,
Why scorn the Duchess's stumbling start?
'When she learned at last he needed her,
The dear knowledge filled and tamed her heart.'

Oh, bury me where the blue begins,
Where ball meets bat as lord meets lord,
Out where the home team always wins
And virtue is its Humphry Ward.

THE STRANGE CASE OF THE LOVELORN LETTER WRITER

Dear Miss Dix, I am a young lady of Scandinavia
origin, and I am in a quandary.
I am not exactly broody, but I am kind of pondery.
I got a twenty-five waist and a thirty-five bust,
And I am going with a chap whose folks are very upper
crust.
He is the intellectual type, which I wouldn't want t
disparage,
Because I understand they often ripen into love afte
marriage,
But here I am all set
For dalliance,
And what do I get?
Shilly-shalliance.
Just when I think he 's going to disrobe me with his eyes
He gets up off the davenport and sighs.
Every time I let down my hair,
He starts talking to himself or the little man who isn't there
Every time he ought to be worrying about me,
Why, he 's worrying about his mother, that 's my mother
in-law to be,
And I say let 's burn that bridge when we come to it
and he says don't I have any sin sense,
His uncle and her live in incense.
Well, with me that 's fine,
Let them go to their church and I'll go to mine.
But no, that 's not good enough for Mr Conscience an
his mental indigestion,
He 's got to find two answers for every question.

If a man is a man, a girl to him is a girl, if I correctly
rememma,
But to him I am just a high pathetical dilemma.
What I love him in spite of
Is, a girl wants a fellow to go straight ahead like a
locomotive and he is more like a loco-might-of.
Dear Miss Dix, I surely need your advice and solace.
It's like I was in love with Henry Wallace.
Well, while I eagerly await your reply I'm going down
to the river to pick flowers. I'll get some rose-
mary if I can't find a camellia.
Yours truly, Orphelia.

Let us all point an accusing finger at Mr Latour.
Mr Latour is an illiterate boor.
He watches horse racing, instead of the sport of kings, when at the track,
And to him first base is simply first base, instead of the initial sack.
He eats alligator pear instead of avocado,
He says fan, or enthusiast, instead of *aficionado*.
He has none of the feeling for words that Ouïda and Spinoza felt,
Instead of Eleanor, he says Mrs Roosevelt.
Sometimes he speaks even more bluntly and rashly,
And says the former Mrs Douglas Fairbanks Senior, or the ex-Mrs Clark Gable, instead of Sylvia, Lady Ashley.
He drinks his drinks in a saloon instead of a tavern or grill,
And pronounces Know-how, skill.
He calls poor people poor, instead of underprivileged,
Claiming that the English language is becoming over-driveleged.
He says the English language ought to get out of the nursery and leave the toys room,
So he goes to the bathroom instead of the little boys' room.
I will offer the hand of my daughter and half my income tax to him who will bring me the head of Mr Latour on a saucer
Before he has everybody else talking as illiterate as Defoe and Chaucer.

HOW TO GET ALONG WITH YOURSELF

or

I RECOMMEND SOFTENING OF THE OUGHTERIES

When I was young I always knew
The meretricious from the true.
I was alert to call a halt
On other people's every fault.
My creed left no more chance for doubt
Than station doors marked IN and OUT.
A prophet with righteousness elated,
Dogmatic and opinionated,
Once self-convinced, I would not budge;
I was indeed a hanging judge.
I admitted, in either joy or sorrow,
No yesterday and no to-morrow.
My summary of life was reckoned
By what went on that very second.
I scoffed when kindly uncles and aunts
Said age would teach me tolerance,
For tolerance implies a doubt
That IN is IN and OUT is OUT.
But now that I am forty-nine
I'm tolerant, and like it fine.
Since the faults of others I condone,
I can be tolerant of my own.
I realize the sky won't fall
If I don't pay my bills at all.
The King of Sweden it will not irk
To hear that I neglect my work,

And tombfuls of historic dead
Care not how late I lie abed.
Oh, tolerance is the state of grace
Where everything falls into place,
So now I tolerantly think
I could tolerate a little drink.

HOW HIGH IS UP?

A SORT OF CHANTEY

Yo heave ho!
Blow the man down, Johnny!
Yo heave ho!
Blow him out of town, Johnny!
Heave yo heave!
Gangway, stairway!
Heave yo heave!
Heave him on the airway!
Fly away, Johnny!
Fly, bonnie Johnny!

The last thing I remembers, I drunk with Deadeye Dick,
My throat is full of embers, and my tongue is tarnal
thick.
I gulps my penicillin for to clarify my brain,
And discovers I am shanghaied on a airyplane.

Oh, maybe I am headed for Cathay or Caroline;
God grant it ain't the corner of Hollywood and Vine!
They have battened down the hatches and I cannot see
a thing
But the high tension wires and a section of the wing.

Yo heave ho!
Feel the rudder wag, Johnny!
Yo heave ho!
Where's the paper bag, Johnny!

Heave yo heave!
Flying men is hardier!
Heave yo heave!
Gander and La Guardia!
Fly away, Johnny!
Fly, bonnie Johnny!

How Nature hastes to welcome the conqueror of space!
How fog and ice enclasp it in rapturous embrace!
This contraption is a triumph of man's inventive wit,
The very mountains skip like rams to get in front of it.

Oh, now the lordly agent, outbargaining the sun,
Can eat his lunch at Chasen's and dine at Twenty-one.
Who that has rode this comet of aluminum and plywood
Would prefer an upper berth behind a grimy choo-choo?
I would.

Yo heave ho!
Blow the man down, Johnny!
Yo heave ho!
Blow him out of town, Johnny!
Heave yo heave!
Heave him in the stratosphere!
Heave yo heave!
Chesterfields they satisphere!
Fly away, Johnny!
Fly, bonnie Johnny!

HOW TO BE MARRIED WITHOUT A SPOUSE

or

MR KIPLING, WHAT HAVE YOU DONE WITH MR HAUKSBEE?

Do any of you old fogies remember Mrs Hauksebe?
Without Mrs Hauksbee, Simla and Poona
Would have been just like Altoona.
At Mrs Hauksbee's *burra khanas*
Nabobs pinned tails on donkeys and viceroys bobbed for bananas.
Mrs Hauksbee disentangled subalterns and aides-de-camp
From shopworn maids-de-camp.
Mrs Hauksbee could rock India with one jab
In the Punjab.
Under the deodars, whatever they may be, Mrs Hauksbee was in her glory,
But this is another story.
Mrs Hauksbee was attended by a faithful old *amah*,
Which is the equivalent of in Alabama a faithful old *mamah*,
And this now *amah* was a conservative reactionary Hindu,
And she got tired of Mrs Hauksbee all the time shifting her hemline and her hair-do and her skin-do,
And finally she asked Mrs Hauksbee why she had dyed her hair again and she got one of the usual answers.

Mrs Hauksbee said she was changing her style to reform
young Slingsby of the Umpteenth Lancers,
And the *amah* (she had surreptitiously attended the
Sorbonne)
Murmured: 'Plus ça change, plus c'est la memsahib,'
and wandered on.

HAVE A SEAT BEHIND THE POTTED PALM, SIR

I'm just an untutored travelling man,
And I only know as much as I can,
But ask me about itineraries,
And I'll tell you one factor that never varies:
All of the overnight trains arrive
In the dim-lit neighbourhood of five.
Wherever you come, from wherever you've gone,
You always get into town at dawn.
You're reluctant to sway to the washroom once
more
Between quivering curtain and quavering snore;
Why should one, when one in one's pocket hath
A hotel reservation for room and bath?
Detroit, Seattle, Dubuque, New Haven,
You descend at sunrise unbuttoned, unshaven,
In yesterday's socks and yesterday's shirt,
And yesterday's city's pervasive dirt,
But only a jiffy, you fondly suppose,
From a bath and a nap and a change of clothes,
Seeing you hold what is laughingly termed
A hotel reservation, confirmed.
You approach the desk with footstep glad,
And your reservation ironclad.
The clerk offhandedly waves you aside;
Your room is there, but it's occupied.
No use to wheedle, nobody to placate;
You're marooned till the squatter decides to vacate.
You retire to a crowded bench in the lobby,
And pretend that your beard is a lovable hobby.

By noon you're a vagrant, offensive and jailable
You're finally told that your room is available.
You ascend to your castle among the stars,
And what do you find? Four dead cigars,
Towels and sheets in a crumpled bunch,
And word that the maid is out to lunch.
By confirmed reservations I'm stymied and bunkered;
I'd just as soon trust a confirmed drunkard.

HEY, HEY FOR THE AMERICAN WAY

The Founding Fathers were men of outstanding talents,
And they founded our system of check and balance,
But you have to discover things before you can found them,
So they discovered the system of check and balance by looking around them,
Thus proving to their own satisfaction
That every action has its equal reaction.
Why do dog-owners grow thin?
Because a dog has to scratch the door to get out so he can turn around and scratch to get in.
Tit is always equal to tat,
And the hopeful relief of a family moving from a flat to a house is balanced by the hopeful relief of a family moving from a house to a flat.
Facts are things that there is no reply to them,
And it is a fact that the active bliss of greeting guests leads to the reactive bliss of saying good-bye to them,
And that is why the Founding Fathers celebrated the discovery of action and reaction with a couple of beers or so,
And gave us the system of checks and balances in which the Republicans are equal to the Democrats, at least every twenty-four years or so.

THE BAT

Myself, I rather like the bat,
It's not a mouse, it's not a rat.
It has no feathers, yet has wings,
It's quite inaudible when it sings.
It zigzags through the evening air
And never lands on ladies' hair,
A fact of which men spend their lives
Attempting to convince their wives.

THE CHIPMUNK

My friends all know that I am shy,
But the chipmunk is twice as shy as I.
He moves with flickering indecision
Likes stripes across the television.
He's like the shadow of a cloud,
Or Emily Dickinson read aloud.
Yet his ultimate purpose is obvious, very:
To get back to his chipmonastery.

THE GRYNCH

I dearly love the three-toed grynch,
It grows upon me inch by inch.
Each home with one should be provided;
The Lord did not create it, so I did.
It's useful for closing conversations
With stubborn salesmen and poor relations.
Long-winded storytellers flinch
If I bring up the three-toed grynch.
When I speak of the grynch which I adore
I'm a bore, I'm a bore, I'm a fabulous bore.
But so can life be; in a pinch,
I recommend the three-toed grynch.

LET'S NOT PLAY LOTTO, LET'S JUST TALK

If anybody says conversation in our day is as good as it was in Dr Johnson's,
Why, that's a lot of nonsense.
The art of conversation has been lost, or at least mislaid,
And no modern phrase-coiner can think of a fresher word for spade than spade.
Take the causerie of the most effervescent coterie,
It sounds like something sworn to before a notary.
Where are yesterday's epigrams, banter, and badinage?
All you hear is who behaved scandalously at the club dance and how hard it is to get a new car into an old garage.
The maxim, the apothegm, yes, even the aphorism, die like echoes in the distance,
Overwhelmed by such provocative topics as clothes, beauticians, taxes, and the scarcity of competent domestic assistants.
Come, sprinkle ashes and coffee substitutes upon my head,
I weep for the art of conversation, it is dead.
But wait a minute, the art of conversation is not dead, see it arise, vigorous, stimulating, and untroubled,
Just as you start to play six spades, vulnerable, doubled and redoubled.

TWEEDLEDEE AND TWEEDLEDOOM

Said the Undertaker to the Overtaker,
Thank you for the butcher and the candlestick-maker,
For the polo player and the pretzel-baker,
For the lawyer and the lover and the wife-forsaker,
Thank you for my bulging, verdant acre,
Said the Undertaker to the Overtaker.
Move in, move under, said the Overtaker.

I REMEMBER YULE

I guess I am just an old fogey.
I guess I am headed for the last round-up, so come along little dogey.
I can remember when winter was wintery and summer was estival;
I can even remember when Christmas was a family festival.
Yes, I can remember when Christmas was an occasion for fireside rejoicing and general goodwill,
And now it is just the day that it's only X shopping days until.
I can remember when we knew Christmas was coming without being reminded by the sponsor
And the annoncer.
What, five times a week at 8.15 p.m., do the herald angels sing?
That a small deposit now will buy you an option on a genuine diamond ring.
What is the message we receive with Good King Wenceslaus?
That if we rush to the corner of Ninth and Main we can get that pink mink housecoat very inexpenceslaus.
I know what came upon the midnight clear to our backward parents, but what comes to us?
A choir imploring us to Come all ye faithful and steal a 1939 convertible at psychoneurotic prices from Grinning Gus.
Christmas is a sitting duck for sponsers, it's so commercial,
And yet so noncontroversial.

Well, you reverent sponsors redolent of frankincense
and myrrh, come smear me with bear-grease and
call me an un-American hellion,
This is my declaration of independence and rebellion.
This year I 'm going to disconnect everything electrical
in the house and spend the Christmas season like
Tiny Tim and Mr Pickwick;
You make me sickwick.

KIPLING'S VERMONT

The summer like a rajah dies,
And every widowed tree
Kindles for Congregational eyes
An alien suttee.

M. C. LOVES T.V.

or

A PERSONALITY IS BORN

I have one kindly kamerad, I have one true amigo,
Who made me what I am to-day, my supersonic ego.
I can't enjoy July the Fourth unless I'm Uncle Sam,
Ham that I am.
As Boston thinks of Bunker Hill, as Richmond thinks of
  Lee,
As Moscow thinks of Uncle Joe, that's how I think of
  me,
An unprecedented wow, like chlorophyll or Boulder
  Dam,
Ham that I am.
I shudder for my parents when I think that maybe
Instead of me they might have had some other baby.
I congratulated mother in a telegram,
Ham that I am.

When bothered by the common cold, the fever, and
  the chills,
The common man takes aspirin, but I need wonder
  pills;
I shiver like Alaska, I perspire like Alabam,
Ham that I am.
I have a native courtliness that nothing can embarrass,
My accent when I eat at Child's transforms it into
  Paris,
I call the waiters garçon and the hostesses Madame,
Ham that I am.

I'm delighted with my country and I've often said it,
A nation that produced myself deserves much credit.
I'm the maraschino cherry in the cherrystone clam,
Ham that I am.

I wrote a lot of operas that were stolen by Puccini,
I wrote the *Canterbury Tales* while sipping a Martini,
I wrote *The Rubáiyát* and signed it Omar Khayyám,
Ham that I am.
Instead of simple business cards I've illustrated folders,
I keep a mermaid in my tub to scrub between my
shoulders,
My taste is so developed I put caviare on jam,
Ham that I am.
It's obvious a genius of my wit and wisdom
Is called upon to entertain the Solar System.
Compared to me a Barrymore is just a bashful lamb,
Ham that I am,
That I am.

MAX SCHLING, MAX SCHLING, LEND ME YOUR GREEN THUMB

A TRAVELOGUE OF FLOWERY CATALOGUES

Bobolink!
Bobolink!
Spink!
Spank!
Spink!
Bobbink!
Atkink!
Sprink!

Burpee.

IT'S ABOUT TIME

How simple was the relationship between the sexes in the days of Francesca di Rimini;
Men were menacing, women were womeny.
When confronted with women, men weren't expected to understand them;
Their alternatives were, if rejected, to un-hand, if accepted, to hand them.
I attribute much of our modern tension
To a misguided striving for intersexual comprehension.
It's about time to realize, brethren, as best we can,
That a woman is not just a female man.
How bootless, then, to chafe
When they are late because they have no watch with them, all eleven of their watches are on the dressing-table or in the safe;
How fruitless to pout
When you can never follow the clues in your detective story because they believe that every time the dog scratches, it really wants to go out;
Bear it and grin
When having been silent all day they time their telephone calls to coincide with Groucho Marx and Ed Wynn;
Give your tongue to the cat
When you ask what they want for their birthday and they say, Oh anything, and you get anything, and then discover it should have been anything but that.
Above all, don't behave like a Monsieur Verdoux
Merely because after spending two hours arranging

themselves to attract you they don't want you to succumb to their attraction because then you would disarrange their lipstick or hairdo.
Pocket the gold, fellows, ask not why it glisters;
As Margaret Fuller accepted the universe, so let us accept her sisters.
Women would I think be easier nationalized
Than rationalized,
And the battle of the sexes can be a most enjoyable scrimmage
If you'll only stop trying to create woman in your own image.

MAYBE YOU CAN'T TAKE IT WITH YOU, BUT LOOK WHAT HAPPENS WHEN YOU LEAVE IT BEHIND

As American towns and cities I wander through,
One landmark is constant everywhere I roam;
The house that the Banker built in nineteen-two,
Dim neon tells me is now a funeral home.

IS IT TRUE WHAT THEY SAY ABOUT DIXIE or IS IT JUST THE WAY THEY SAY IT?

Our country, south and west of Hatteras,
Abounds in charming feminine flatteras.
Sweet talk is scant by Lake Cayuga,
But in Tennessee, they chatta nougat.

Come, child, while rambling through the nation
Let's practise our pronunciation.
The liquid confluence here we see
Of r-i-b and a-l-d.
When first potato chips he nibbled,
That gentleman was merely ribald,
But now that he is four-rye-highballed,
We may properly pronounce him ribald.

LECTURER IN BOOKSTORE

Behold best-selling Mr Furneval,
Behind a pile of books to autograph,
Like a bearded lady at a carnival
Hoping to sell her fly-specked photograph.

THE DUST STORM

or

I'VE GOT TEXAS IN MY LUNGS

Nobody minds
Dust storms in Lubbock;
They don't create havoc,
Just hubbubbock.
But I'm so full
Of Holy Texas
I'll be hallowed ground
When they annex us.

REFLECTION ON THE VERNACULAR

In cooking *petits pois*, or lesser peas,
Some use receipts, and some use recipes.
In spite of opposition warm,
I choose to use the former form.
In fact, though you may think me gossipy,
I plan to settle near Lake Ossipee,
When my arrangements are complete
To change its name to Lake Osseipt.

I CAN'T STOP UNLESS YOU STOP

or

LINES ADDRESSED TO A MAN MAKING $5,000 A YEAR WHO OVERTIPS A MAN MAKING $10,000 A YEAR TO MAKE HIMSELF FEEL HE'S MAKING $20,000 A YEAR

I do not wish to tiptoe through the tulips to Tipperary,
And I might vote for Tyler too, but about Tippecanoe I am a little wary.
The fact is, that at any mention of any form of tips,
My mind goes into an eclipse.
The world of tips has moved too fast for me,
The price of ransoming my hat has become too vast for me.
I have to get used to one thing at a time,
And just as I learn that there is no more such tip as a nickel, I find that there is no more such tip as a dime.
If you give a dime to a bellhop,
The skyscrapers buck like broncos, and you can almost feel the hotel hop.
If you want to talk to bellhops or porters,
You start with baby-talk, which is quarters.
If you want to talk to head waiters, or, as they now style themselves, Maitre d's,
You talk in C's or G's,

And the girl with the tray of cigarettes expects the Taj Mahal,
And not a small Mahal, either, but a large Mahal.
This is a sad situation for low and middle income persons,
And when you go abroad, it worsens.
At least on the trains over here
You don't have to tip the conductor and the engineer,
And over here, certainly until recently, it would have been considered impudent effrontery
To tip the President of the country,
Whereas, in certain nations that shall be nameless,
The entire citizenry is shameless.
Granted that itching palms
Know no qualms,
Nevertheless people, whether men or mice,
Resent scratching the same palm twice,
Which happens wherever you eat or sleep, on the continent, because a fat percentage is added to the bill to cover all tips,
But if you think that no further tipping is expected, you'd better learn to carry your own pemmican and balance your baggage on your hips.
Oh dear, I think that extravagant tips are an unnecessary menace,
Whether in Valdosta, Georgia, or Valparaiso, or Vancouver, or Venice.
I think that they are a betrayal of the tipper's unsure ego, or not quite-quiteness,
I think that they are a vulgar substitute for common politeness.

I think that people could do very well both at home
and abroad on moderate gratuities or fees
If they would just take the trouble to learn and employ
the foreign and domestic terms for Thank you
and Please.

YOU CAN'T TELL THE HIT PARADE WITHOUT A DRUM MAJORETTE

In Africa, it's the sirocco.
Our equivalent is the disk jocko.

The jocko's chatter is brisk,
Four commercials to every disk.

The commercials are Brahmses and Bachs
Compared to the disks he jocks.

For instance, he cannot assuage
His passion for Patti Page,

That perhaps too talented elf
Who sings quartets by herself.

Thanks to scientific genius,
She sings four parts simulteneous.

If snowbound alone on a ridge,
I suppose she could always play bridge,

But such multiple schizophrenia
Is a vocal misdemeanior.

Yet nothing delights the disk jocko
Like Patti's quadruple echo.

Her effect on disk jockos is radical,
Like blackstrap molasses or Hadacol;

They will even curtail their chatter
To spin you her recentest platter.

What will hold me through Patti and the commercial
It's only my middle-aged inertia'll.

Thus grumbles this radio kibitzer,
But I doubt that I jolt the jock diskers.
My opinions are flibberty-gibbertzer,
And Coolidge peeks out through my whiskers.

THE LEPIDOPTERIST

The lepidopterist with happy cries
Devotes his days to hunting butterflies.
The leopard, through some feline mental twist,
Would rather hunt a lepidopterist.
That's why I never adopted lepidoptery;
I do not wish to live in jeopardoptery.

THIS IS MY OWN, MY NATIVE TONGUE

Often I leave my television set to listen to my wireless,
So, often I hear the same song sung by the same singer many times a day, because at repeating itself the wireless is tireless.
There is one such song from which at sleepy time I can hardly bear to part,
A song in which this particular singer, who apparently has offended a nameless character in an undescribed way, states that he apawlogizes from the bawttom of his heart.
I am familiar with various accents—I know that in Indiana you stress the ' r ' in Carmen,
And that in Georgia if a ladybug's house is on far she sends for the farmen,
And I have paaked my caah in Cambridge, and elsewhere spoken with those who raise hawgs and worship strange gawds—but here I am, late in life's autumn,
Suddenly confronted with somebody's apawlogies and bawttom.
I tell you whawt,
Things were different when I was a tawddling tawt.
I may have been an indifferent schawlar,
Lawling around in my blue serge suit and doodling on my Eton cawllar;
In fact, I didn't even pick up much knawledge
In a year at cawllege;
I guess that of normal intelligence I had only about two thirds,
But, by gum, I was taught, or, by gum, was I tot, to pronounce my words.

And now they've gawt me wondering:
Was it the dawn or the don that from China cross the bay came up thundering?
As a tot, was I tawddling or was I toddling?
When I doodled, was I dawdling or was I dodling?
I have forgawtten oll I ever knew of English, I find my position as an articulate mammal bewildering and awesome.
Would God I were a tender apple blawssom.

LOVE ME BUT LEAVE MY DOG ALONE

Once there was a handsome man named Mr Beamington
    and he was to good causes the most generous of
    donors,
And he was so popular with dogs that he couldn't
    understand why he was so unpopular with their
    owners.
He was bold as an eagle, a cock eagle, yet gentle as a
    dove, a hen-dove,
And the dog didn't live that he couldn't make a friend
    of.
If you had a brace of ferocious spaniels
Mr Beamington would soon be romping with them
    through your annuals and peranniels.
He fondled schnauzers
With no scathe to his trousers.
At his voice the pit bull eschewed the manners of the
    bull pit,
And assumed those of the pulpit.
He could discuss Confucianism with a Pekinese,
And address the Boston terrier on Beacon Hill in purest
    Beaconese.
Yes, Mr Beamington had a way with dogs, dogs simply
    adored him,
Yet their owners abhorred him,
Because he reckoned without the third law of Para-
    celsus,
Which clearly states that every dog-owner considers his
    dog a one-man dog, and its affection his own and
    nobody elsus.

So the only people who liked him were the owners of a Cairn,
Which frequently bit him, thus reassuring them that its heart was not hisn but theirn.

LIMERICK ONE

An elderly bride of Port Jervis
Was quite understandably nervis,
Since her apple-cheeked groom,
With three wives in the tomb,
Kept insuring her during the service.

LIMERICK TWO

There was a young lady of Guam
Who peddled her charms, charm by charm,
Inspired, I suppose,
By the classical prose
Of W. Somerset Maugham.

LIMERICK THREE

A lady from near Rising Sun,
She flattened her boy friend in fun,
Saying, Don't worry kid,
That's for nothing you did,
It's for something I dreamt that you done.

JUST PRESS THE BUTTON, THE BUTTON-HOLE IS REALLY A DEEPFREEZE

You ask the cause, madam, of my agitation?
Gadgetation.
I am one who found sufficient duplicity
In plain old electricity;
Now that it has become electronics,
My vapours are chronics.
I am just a modest student of householdology,
Not a graduate of the Massachusetts or California Institutes of Technology.
Once I was master in my own home, and my family's hearts with pride went hippity-hoppit,
Because when the plumbing kept on running I knew how to lift the lid of the tank and twiddle with the ball, and stop it.
To-day my satellites are rather less sycophantic than Saturn's
Simply because when I touch the television I get nothing but herringbone and sharkskin patterns;
I am no longer the Old Man, He Who Sees All and Knows All,
I am only He Who Put the Bubble Gum in the Dispose-All.
The scientists are so far out in front of each other that even my bedclothes croon,
Ignoring which, I shall put myself to sleep with my dog-eared copy of *Tom Swift and His Wonderful Illuminating Gas Balloon.*

IT WAS NOT I WHO POSED FOR RODIN

or

WHY I FLUNKED PHILOSOPHY IV

Once you really get thinking about thinking,
It's worse than drinking.
You begin to think that because you think, you exist,
And you proceed to think that anything not thought about by you has no more existence than the clench after you have unclenched your fist.
You become so involved in the spirit
That you think a noise is not a noise unless you are there to hear it,
And speaking of noise, by this time you are thinking so dreamily
That you think your voice when you listen to it in the bath-tub rings out Wagnerianly, or at least Frimly.
Your id is now cooking with iridium;
You think that a couple of Martinis improve your French in both accent and idiom.
The only trouble is that the French have been thinking, too,
And they think faster than you,
Which they naturally have to by at least two thirds
Just to keep up with their own words,
Because you may be the language-ropin' champion of Texas, mah deah suh,
But still they can say: '*Qu'est-ce que c'est que ça*,' quicker than you can say: 'Huh?'

Nevertheless, I think that nothing is but thinking makes it so,
And I intend to take two Martinis and sing 'Frère Jacques' in my bath and think the French into talking slow.

TUNE FOR AN ILL-TEMPERED CLAVICHORD

Oh, once there lived in Kankakee
A handy dandy Yankakee,
A lone and lean and lankakee
Cantankakerous Yankakee.
He slept without a blankaket,
And whisky, how he drankaket,
This rough and ready Yankakee,
The bachelor of Kankakee.
He never used a hankakee,
He jeered at hanky-pankakee;
Indeed, to give a frank account,
He didn't have a bank account.
And yet at times he hankakered
In marriage to be anchachored.
When celibacy rankakles,
One dreams of pretty ankakles.
He took a trip to Waikiki
And wooed a girl named Psycheche,
And now this rugged Yankakee
'S a married man in Kankakee.
Good night, dear friends, and thankakee.

INDEX OF FIRST LINES